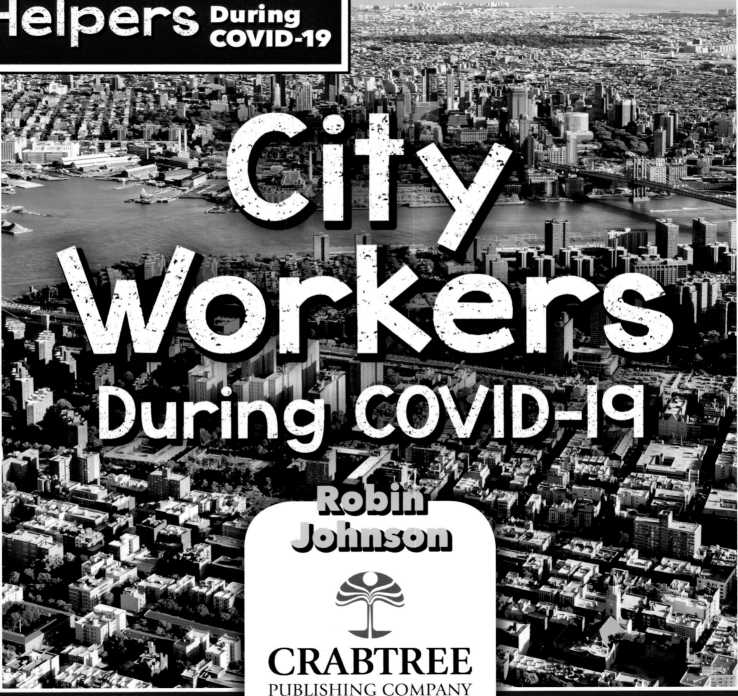

Community Helpers During COVID-19

City Workers During COVID-19

Robin Johnson

CRABTREE
PUBLISHING COMPANY
WWW.CRABTREEBOOKS.COM

CRABTREE
PUBLISHING COMPANY
WWW.CRABTREEBOOKS.COM

Author: Robin Johnson
Series research and development:
  Janine Deschenes
Editorial director: Kathy Middleton
Editor: Janine Deschenes
Proofreader: Melissa Boyce
Graphic design: Katherine Berti
Image research: Robin Johnson
Print coordinator: Katherine Berti

Images:
Alamy
   ITAR-TASS News Agency: p. 18 (bottom)
   SFM Press Reporter: p. 7 (top)
Shutterstock
   ArCere: p. 3 (police car)
   Chadolfski: p. 20 (top), 23 (top right)
   Dziurek: p. 20 (bottom)
   Irina Sen: p. 3 (taxi)
   Kilmer Media: p. 22–23 (top)
   lev radio: p. 8 (bottom), 11 (top)
   Mike Dotta: p. 15 (top)
   Ned Snowman: p. 9
   Shawn Goldberg: p. 6 (top)
   Thomas Koch: p. 10 (bottom)
All other images by Shutterstock

Library and Archives Canada Cataloguing in Publication

Title: City workers during COVID-19 / Robin Johnson.
Names: Johnson, Robin (Robin R.), author.
Description: Series statement: Community helpers during COVID-19 |
   Includes index.
Identifiers: Canadiana (print) 20200390872 |
   Canadiana (ebook) 20200390880 |
   ISBN 9781427128317 (hardcover) |
   ISBN 9781427128355 (softcover) |
   ISBN 9781427128393 (HTML)
Subjects: LCSH: COVID-19 (Disease)–Juvenile literature. |
   LCSH: Service industries workers–Juvenile
 literature. | LCSH: Epidemics–Social aspects–Juvenile literature. |
   LCSH: Community life–Juvenile literature.
Classification: LCC RA644.C67 J64 2021 | DDC j614.5/92414–dc23

Library of Congress Cataloging-in-Publication Data

Available at the Library of Congress

Crabtree Publishing Company
www.crabtreebooks.com   1-800-387-7650

Printed in the U.S.A./012021/CG20201112

**Published
in Canada**
Crabtree Publishing
616 Welland Ave.
St. Catharines, Ontario
L2M 5V6

**Published in the
United States**
Crabtree Publishing
347 Fifth Ave.
Suite 1402-145
New York, NY 10016

**Published in the
United Kingdom**
Crabtree Publishing
Maritime House
Basin Road North, Hove
BN41 1WR

**Published
in Australia**
Crabtree Publishing
Unit 3 - 5 Currumbin Court
Capalaba
QLD 4157

Contents

From City to City 4

Community Helpers 6

City Builders 8

First Responders 10

Teachers and Librarians 12

Transportation Workers 14

Energy Workers 16

Water Workers 18

Community Cleaners 20

Glossary 22

Index 23

About the Author 23

Notes to Parents and Educators 24

From City to City

In 2019, a **disease** called COVID-19 began to make people sick. The disease spread quickly from person to person. Soon there was a **pandemic**. This means it spread all around the world.

COVID-19 spread through cities around the world.

In some places, parks and many other **public** areas were closed to stop people from gathering in groups.

*This worker is getting his **temperature** checked to see if he is sick.*

The leaders of countries and cities have made rules to keep people safe. They say people should wash their hands often. They should wear face masks in public places. They should not get too close to other people.

In some places, leaders decided that there should be a **lockdown** for a period of time. This meant that many places, such as schools, were closed. People had to stay home as much as possible.

Community Helpers

Some people cannot stay home during the pandemic. City workers need to keep their communities running. A community is a group of people who live, work, and play in the same area.

These city workers are ready to help their community.

Postal workers are an important part of communities. They deliver letters, paychecks, packages, and other mail.

People in every community have **basic needs** that must be met. They need food and clean water. They need places to live. They need to travel safely from place to place. Brave city workers make sure people can still meet their needs.

Workers try to keep COVID-19 from spreading through city jails.

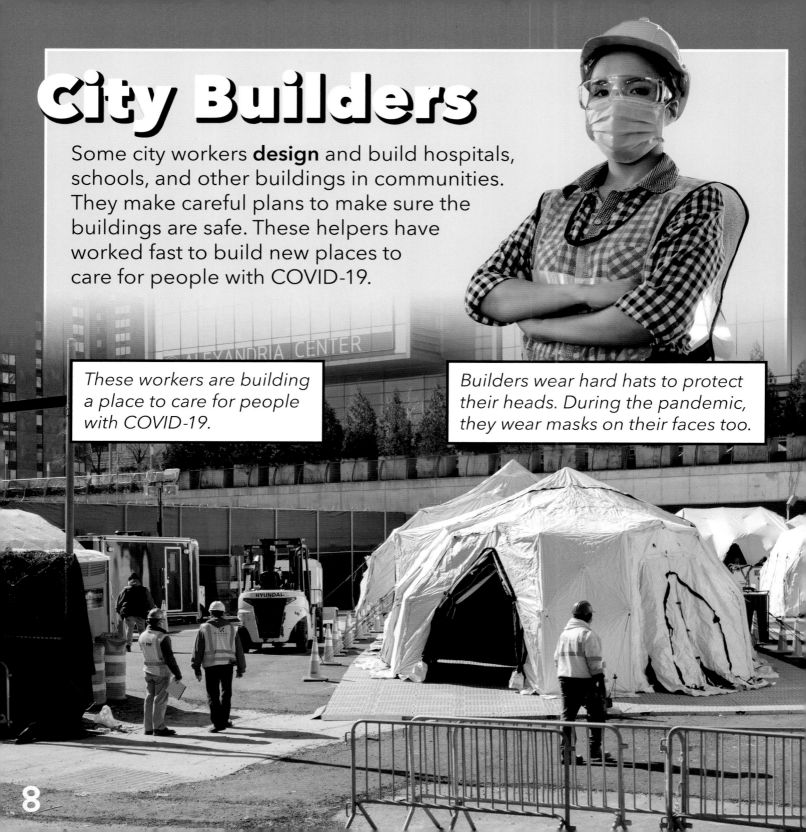

City Builders

Some city workers **design** and build hospitals, schools, and other buildings in communities. They make careful plans to make sure the buildings are safe. These helpers have worked fast to build new places to care for people with COVID-19.

These workers are building a place to care for people with COVID-19.

Builders wear hard hats to protect their heads. During the pandemic, they wear masks on their faces too.

8

Other city workers build and repair roads. Communities need good roads during the pandemic. Truck drivers use roads to deliver food and supplies. Helpers use roads to take sick people to hospitals.

City workers fix bumps and holes in the roads. They also fix pipes and wires under the roads.

First Responders

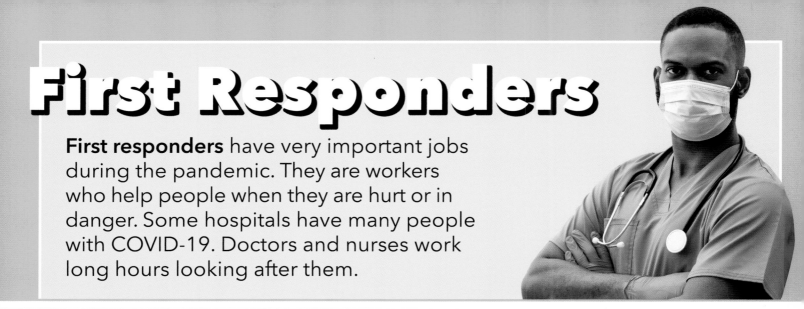

First responders have very important jobs during the pandemic. They are workers who help people when they are hurt or in danger. Some hospitals have many people with COVID-19. Doctors and nurses work long hours looking after them.

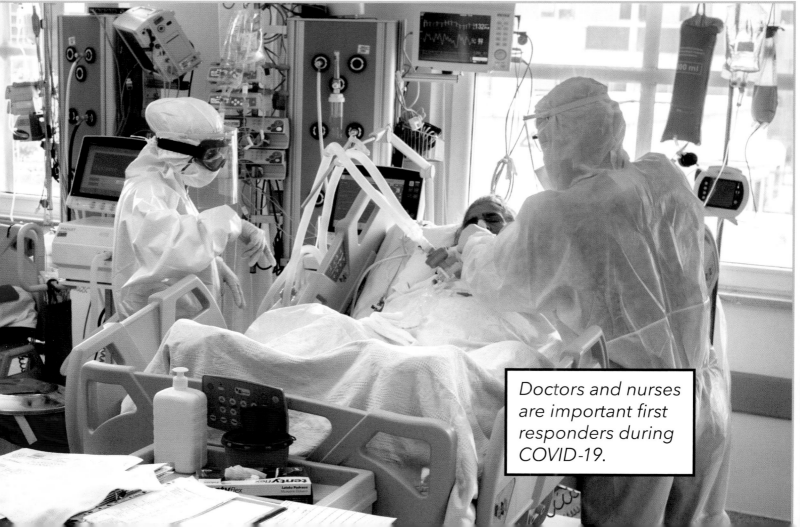

Doctors and nurses are important first responders during COVID-19.

This police officer makes sure people follow the rules in a city park.

Police officers are first responders too. They help keep people safe. During the pandemic, police have made sure people follow all the new rules. They tell people to wear masks and stay a safe distance apart. They make sure people do not gather in large groups.

Firefighters are first responders who have helped others during the pandemic. They rescue people from fires. They also help people who are sick or hurt.

13

Teachers and Librarians

Many schools were closed during lockdowns to keep people safe. Teachers taught classes from their computers, however. They recorded lessons and talked to students online. When schools opened, teachers worked hard to keep their classrooms safe.

Teachers set up their classrooms so students do not get too close to each other. They wear masks and clean their rooms carefully.

Some families chose to keep students at home to stay safe. Teachers continue to give online lessons to these students.

Libraries were also closed during lockdowns. But librarians kept people reading! People could order books and pick them up outside some libraries. They could also read many library books online.

When libraries opened, librarians carefully cleaned shelves and other **surfaces**. They make sure people can visit safely.

13

This man is taking a bus to get food. Some of the seats are blocked off to keep people apart.

Transportation Workers

Many people still need to get from place to place during the pandemic. Some have to go to work. Others have to get food or go to the hospital. Bus drivers and other city workers make sure everyone can travel safely.

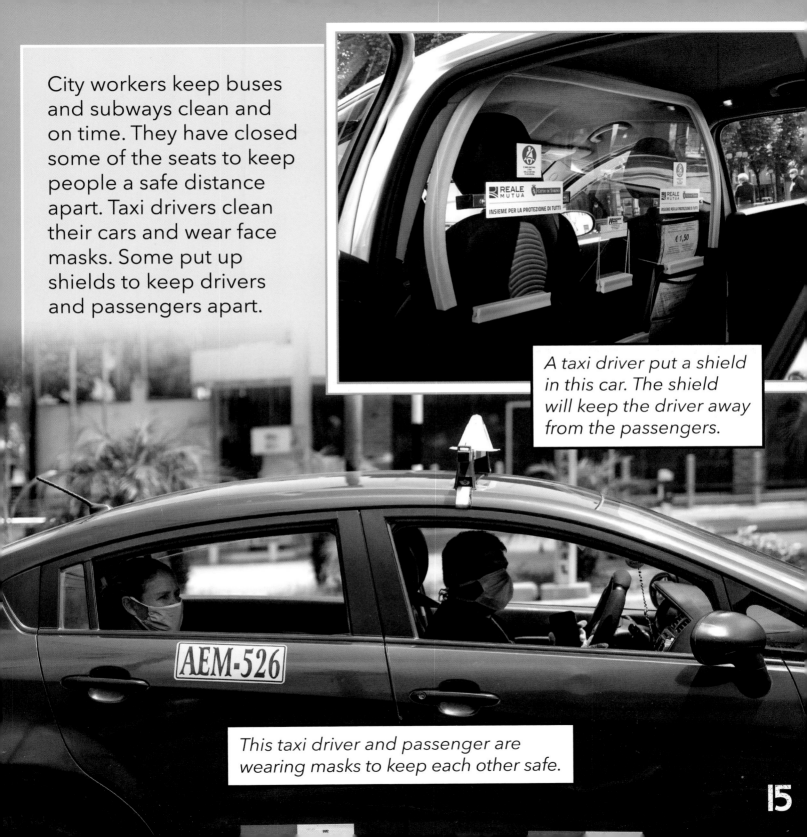

City workers keep buses and subways clean and on time. They have closed some of the seats to keep people a safe distance apart. Taxi drivers clean their cars and wear face masks. Some put up shields to keep drivers and passengers apart.

A taxi driver put a shield in this car. The shield will keep the driver away from the passengers.

This taxi driver and passenger are wearing masks to keep each other safe.

Energy Workers

Some city workers bring **energy** to communities. They bring **fuel** to gas stations so people can drive cars. They bring power to places so people can use lights and computers. They work hard so people can heat and cool their homes.

Helpers work day and night to bring people the power they need.

People need gas or other fuel to run their cars. Workers make sure they can get it.

During the pandemic, people have depended on energy workers more than ever. Many people used computers to work from home. They filled their fridges and freezers with food. Doctors used machines in hospitals. Workers make sure everyone gets the energy they need.

This worker is checking the heating and cooling system in a building.

Water Workers

All people have a basic need for clean water. We need water for drinking and for washing. City workers make sure people can get the clean water they need.

City workers make sure people have clean water to wash their hands.

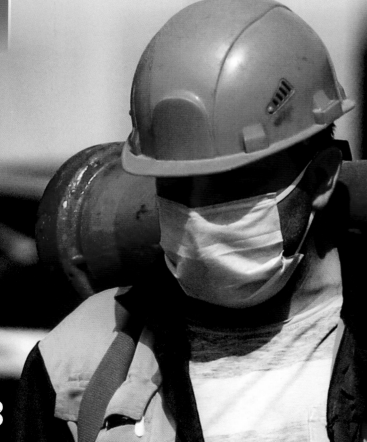

This worker is fixing a water pipe in his community.

*This worker is testing water to make sure it does not **contain** COVID-19.*

Pets need clean water to drink too!

People also need to remove dirty water from homes and other places. Dirty water goes down the drain in sinks, bathtubs, and toilets. Then, city workers clean the dirty water. During the pandemic, they have made sure COVID-19 does not spread in the water.

City workers wear masks and gloves when they clean the streets.

Community Cleaners

It is important to keep communities clean during the pandemic. Some city workers remove garbage that could spread COVID-19. They pick up trash on city streets. They take bags of garbage away from homes each week.

Other workers clean communities from top to bottom. They use strong cleaners that destroy COVID-19. Some wear special suits. The workers clean park benches and bus stops. They clean subways and elevators. They even clean swings and slides!

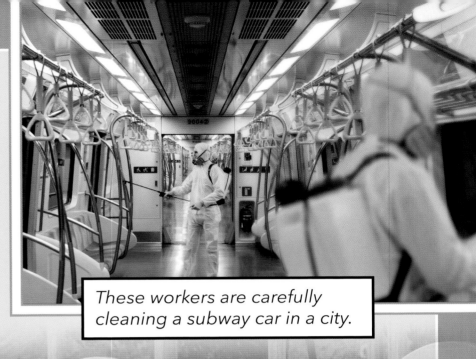

These workers are carefully cleaning a subway car in a city.

This worker is cleaning a playground in a city. He wears a suit to keep him safe.

21

Glossary

basic need Something that people cannot live without

contain To have something inside or within

design To make a plan for how something is made or built

disease A sickness that prevents a person's body from working as it should

energy Power that people can use, such as heat and electricity

first responders People who are trained to help others during an emergency

fuel Material that is burned to create power

lockdown A rule for people to stay where they are

pandemic A disease spreading over the whole world or a very wide area, such as many countries

public Open to everyone

surface The outside or any one side of an object

temperature A measure of how hot or cold something is

Index

bus drivers 14

city jails 7

cleaning
    12–13, 15, 18–21

doctors 10, 17

firefighters 11

lockdown 5, 12–13

nurses 10

parks 4, 11, 21

police officers 11

postal workers 6

power 16–17

roads 9

schools 12–13

taxi drivers 15

water 18–19

About the Author

Robin Johnson is a freelance author and editor who has written more than 100 published children's books. She was fortunate to work from home during the pandemic and is grateful to all the helpers who kept her community running and her family safe.

Notes to Parents and Educators

City Workers During COVID-19 celebrates the brave city workers who are helping members of their communities stay safe, meet their basic needs, and receive services, health care, and education. Below are suggestions to help children make connections and develop their reading and social studies skills.

Before reading

Write down children's answers to the following questions:

- Who are some important people in your community? Why are they important?

Point out people who are city workers. Explain that city workers are people who do jobs that keep cities running.

During reading

After reading pages 10 and 11, turn to the glossary definition of first responders on page 22. Ask children:

- Who are first responders?

- Why are they given that name?

After reading

Explain to children that together, city workers make sure everyone in a community can meet their needs. Then ask children:

- How do you play an important role in your community? What can you do to help others?

Help children understand that every person plays an important role in their community. Make a list of actions, such as wearing a mask, that one can do to help others in their community.